Let's All Sing

MW00979769

COLLECTION FOR YOUNG VOICES

Arranged by Tom Anderson

Disney

THE PRINCESS AND THE FROG

TABLE OF CONTENTS

ISBN 978-1-4234-7606-1

Walt Disney Music Company
Wonderland Music Company, Inc.

DISTRIBUTED BY

HAL•LEONARD®
CORPORATION

7777 W. BLUEMOUND RD. P.O. BOX 13819 MILWAUKEE, WI 53213

Visit Hal Leonard Online at
www.halleonard.com

DOWN IN NEW ORLEANS

Music and Lyrics by RANDY NEWMAN
Arranged by TOM ANDERSON

* If melody is out of range, sing notes in parentheses

2/7

ALMOST THERE

Music and Lyrics by RANDY NEWMAN
Arranged by TOM ANDERSON

* If melody is out of range, sing notes in parentheses.

ev - 'ry - where,__ and I'm al - most there,__ I'm al - most there.__

There's been trials and trib - u - la - tions. You know I've__ had__ my share, but I've

WHEN WE'RE HUMAN

Music and Lyrics by RANDY NEWMAN
Arranged by TOM ANDERSON

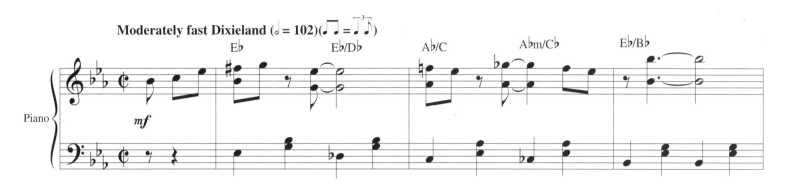

If I were a hu-man be - ing, I'd head straight for New Or - leans,

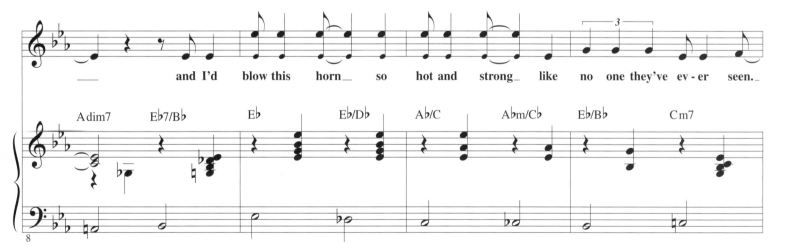

and I'd blow this horn_ so hot and strong_ like no one they've ev - er seen.

* If melody is out of range, sing notes in parentheses.

14

20

MA BELLE EVANGELINE

Music and Lyrics by RANDY NEWMAN
Arranged by TOM ANDERSON

* If melody is out of range, sing notes in parentheses.

22

DIG A LITTLE DEEPER

Music and Lyrics by RANDY NEWMAN
Arranged by TOM ANDERSON

Moderate Gospel 2-Beat (♩ = 98)

Don't mat-ter what you look like, don't mat-ter what you wear.

How man - y rings you got on your fin-ger? We don't care,_ no, we don't care!_

spoken / *All shout*

* If melody is out of range, sing notes in parentheses